safe to love

Understanding Vulnerability to Manipulation

Exploring the Factors That Make Us Susceptible

Kittie Rose

Copyright © 2024 by Kittie Rose

All rights are reserved, and no part of this publication may be reproduced, distributed, or transmitted in any manner, whether through photocopying, recording, or any other electronic or mechanical methods, without the explicit prior written permission of the publisher. This restriction applies to any form or means of reproduction or distribution.

Exceptions to this rule include brief quotations that may be incorporated into critical reviews, as well as certain other noncommercial uses that are allowed by copyright law. Any such usage must adhere to the specified conditions and permissions outlined by the copyright holder.

ISBN 979-8-218-38501-9

Book Design by HMDPUBLISHING

Contents

FACING MYSELF

Introduction 7
I. Making My Way to "The Couch" 9

What Makes Us Susceptible to Manipulation

II. Hello Desperation! 15
III. I Had Excessive Accommodation Syndrome.
Just Kidding, I'm a Recovering People-Pleaser! 24
IV. The Codependent Ties that Bind. 33
V. The Vulnerability of Empathy 41
VI. The Seeds of Doubt 46
VII. No Strings Attached 52

The Profile of the Manipulator

VIII. Sharpening the Untrained Eye 59
IX. Cluster B "The Relationship Destroyer" 63

The Manipulator's Playbook

X. Tactics & Strategies 77

To Overcome and Empower

XI. Consequences of Being Manipulated or
Psychologically Abused 95
XII. Outsmarting the Manipulator 97

Letter from Kittie 101

Part *One*
FACING MYSELF

Introduction

Life is a complex journey, filled with twists and turns that often force us to confront our inner demons. Before I began coaching individuals and couples, on my own personal odyssey, I found myself repeatedly facing the realization that much of my own suffering was self-inflicted. It was a sobering truth to acknowledge the many ways in which I had been complicit in my own pain.

Time and again, I'd find myself grappling with the uncomfortable realization that the seeds of vulnerability to abuse and manipulation were sown deep within my own psyche. For far too long, I blamed the people who took advantage of this vulnerability, failing to recognize my role in giving them the power to do so.

My journey of self-discovery was detailed and marked by countless hours, days, weeks, and years of introspection and soul-searching. Hear me out; introspection was not easy. However, through this process, plus the privilege of working with countless men, women, and couples, I had come to understand the profound impact of my actions and choices. By peeling back the layers of my failures, I had begun to unearth the dormant strength within myself to rewrite my narrative and reclaim agency over my life. I hope you do so as well.

In sharing my story alongside tools from my practice, I hope to offer solace and insight to those ready to free themselves from their self-inflicted pain. By confronting the brutal truths we carry, we can begin to heal and truly experience the joys of liberation.

This is a book to guide you with self-introspection, accountability, and, ultimately, resilience. Welcome to our journey together.

Chapter I.
Making My Way to "The Couch"

Up until 2021, I've operated from a place of low self-worth for as long as I can remember. Instead of facing myself, I tried to rationalize my behaviors by blaming others. I excused their inexcusable behaviors and rationalized their offensive nature because I feared losing them. So afraid of losing people that I would place them on pedestals and prioritize what they needed over my needs. I would give and give to the point of spiritual, emotional, and mental exhaustion just to be loved. I was constantly blaming others for not being able to love me correctly. Although it was true in some instances, most of the time, I continually sought love from unstable or unavailable people. I was constantly trying to prove my worth to both them and me. How much would I do to show and confirm that I am worthy of their love? What would be needed to show I was good enough to be prioritized?

It wasn't until my last tumultuous relationship that I realized that I was giving him the blueprint of how to mistreat and manipulate me. Suppose I elaborated on every detail of that relationship. In that case, you'd probably close this book and take a moment to decompress for me. Trust me, it was a horrible mixture of lies, cheating, gaslighting, devaluation, triangulation, and much more.

However, it all led me to the couch I dreaded for so long. It led me to therapy. While under his wing, my mentor stated, "How can you expect to help anyone if you can't help yourself?" It was a much-needed dose of reality that I was avoiding. I was operating in a victim mentality. It stung like a shot of warm rum after a long day of lies, tears, and heartbreak from a narcissistic avoidant.

The first day I entered therapy, I knew she and I would not be compatible in a client-therapy relationship. However, I gave her a few sessions to see what I could make out of it. While in therapy, I noticed that she had experienced a lot of the same things I had. Here's the unfortunate part, I don't believe she had worked on her trauma enough. It seemed as though there were a lot of generalized statements and trauma from her end. Understand, this is in no way an attempt to bash my previous therapist. I want to help you understand my journey to highlight how I got to feel safe to love so you can do the same.

I wanted to help myself without using others to avoid the accountability I needed to face head-on. I wanted to understand how my thoughts, emotions, and behaviors were repeatedly putting me in the same position. I took my concerns to my mentor, a fantastic psychologist during his time of practice; he is where the real "me" was discovered. He allowed me to study his notes, research, exercises, and recorded therapy sessions. I learned much about how my formative years impacted my perception of myself. In doing so, I learned new and improved ways of helping my clients. I studied, healed, and dedicated my days to creating tools that worked and were easy to use by my clients. I have always had a gift for simplifying things so that people can better comprehend what they are learning. I pride myself on doing the same throughout this book.

Understand that you may have yet to go through each form of manipulation identified in this book, but identifying even the ones you have not experienced and increasing your awareness of the strategies manipulators employ is essential to help you recognize and identify them if they were to present themselves. In a world filled with various people, we may inevitably encounter manipulative behavior at some point. With this understanding, you can create a safer, more genuine space for love to flourish.

Part Two
What Makes Us Susceptible to Manipulation

Chapter II.
Hello Desperation!

Have you ever been on a desperate search for love and acceptance? Ever struggled with feelings of inadequacy or feeling like you're not good enough for the things you deeply desire? Low self-worth can lead us to an ongoing quest for validation. As humans, we want validation outside of the validation we provide ourselves. Still, it becomes concerning when we depend on validation from outside sources, better known as external validation. Believing that we're unworthy of love or respect yet continuing to plead for love and respect from people who show they can't or do not want to provide it should be enough for us to stop and analyze our behaviors. Instead, our desperation for love results in us tolerating unhealthy or abusive relationships, as we believe this is the best we can attract. This cycle of low self-worth and desperate romantic pursuits perpetuates a harmful pattern, further damaging our self-esteem.

We value ourselves low, and each time we accept mistreatment or abuse, we worsen the process of devaluation. Why would we stay with a person who isn't good for us when we have the choice to choose ourselves and leave? Fear. One fear for sure is the fear of being alone. The fear of being alone due to low self-worth can lead us to cling to any sign of affection, regardless of its genuineness or sustainability. As a result, we may continue to enter relationships with incompatible partners or settle for less than we deserve, further perpetuating our feelings of unworthiness.

I worked with a client for about two years, and he struggled with low self-worth and a deep fear of being alone. He was well into his late thirties, married for twelve years without children. He wanted to end his marriage to his abusive wife, but it was quite a challenge. I remember when he would sit on the beige loveseat across from me and become visibly uneasy. When we dug into his thinking patterns, it was evident that he experienced constant self-doubt and a persistent belief that he was unworthy of the love he provided and the respect he desired. This ingrained mindset stemmed from his childhood. His mother, whom he both deeply loved and despised, was controlling and overly critical. Each time he spoke about his wife, he put his head down and shrunk his body onto the couch the same way when he talked about his mother. It was very telling, to say the least. In his childhood and marriage, he was compared to others, and his shortcomings were always emphasized, drowning him with constant complaints and expressions of disapproval and disappointment.

Not to mention, the relationship before his marriage was a mutually verbally and emotionally abusive one. When we walked through his previous relationship, we identified a few things that negatively impacted how he viewed himself and others. His ex-girlfriend exploited his insecurities and used manipulative tactics to maintain a sense of control. She would monitor his friendships and control many variables of his life to help her maintain a sense of security within her inner world. There were ongoing arguments and threats to leave the relationship, which in turn happened within his marriage as well.

In his previous relationship and his marriage, he rationalized each woman's behavior, convincing himself that he didn't deserve better treatment. He would make desperate attempts to prove he was worthy of being loved properly. Both his ex-girlfriend and his wife showed intermittent displays of affection and remorse after aggressive outbursts and abusive manners, offering fleeting moments of validation that my client craved. Because of this, my client relied on each woman for his self-esteem. He sought approval and validation from the very source that undermined his worth. It was almost an eerie reflection of this childhood. It seemed like an endless cycle to him.

Each relationship formed similarly. His longing for affection and validation drove him to seek love in all the wrong places. His desire for love led him to ignore the red flags that peppered his partner's behavior. Both his ex-girlfriend and wife's manipulation and emotional outbursts were often excused in the name of affection, attributing possessiveness to love and control to concern. Hurtful words and belittling remarks became the norm, each apology drenched in tears and pleas for another chance. Over time, he depended on their affection and apologies as validation and reassurance. Their apologies become a temporary fix for the hurt and disappointment they'd caused, leading him to believe that things would change.

Dependency became an obstacle for him when he left his marriage. He repeatedly stated, "Without my wife, I feel lost." Because of the nature of the abuse and several failed marriage counselors, it was proven time for him to leave. It's not uncommon to seek validation from someone who undermines your worth, especially when you've been in a relationship with them for a long time. However, it is essential to remember that your worth isn't determined by anyone else. It comes from within YOU.

It may be hard to believe at times, but that is okay. It is a process that takes time and courage. Now, the million-dollar questions. Is it easy to spot a person with low self-worth? The short answer is yes and no. This can be complex because some people can conceal their feelings behind a façade, and people can compensate by projecting a confident or booming image.

Now, for the people who obviously have low self-worth, these are some of the ways a manipulative, exploitive, or abusive person could identify them:

Constant self-criticism

Suppose you're constantly putting yourself down, excessively criticizing yourself, or have a habit of highlighting your flaws. In this case, it indicates that you may struggle with your self-image. This can look or sound like critical comments about your appearance, abilities, or worthiness of love and affection.

Seeking External Validation

Suppose you constantly seek validation from friends, strangers, or dating/romantic prospects, such as continually needing reassurance about your attractiveness, intelligence, or value. In this case, this can be a huge indicator you're operating from a place of low self-worth.

Difficulty Accepting Compliments or Discounting the Positives

Suppose you downplay or deflect positive feedback or compliments or outright reject them. In this case, this can show a lack of belief in your worthiness. It's almost as if you're wearing a bright yellow sign that says, "I don't believe I am worthy!"

Dependency on the Relationship for Self-Worth

If you struggle with being alone, fear abandonment, or constantly need reassurance or attention from your romantic partner, this dependence on the relationship for self-worth can be noticeable.

Over-Accommodating Behaviors

People with low self-worth often put their partner's needs above their own, struggling to assert their desires and boundaries. Many things are usually done for others at the expense of their own well-being.

> *People with low self-worth often put their partner's needs above their own, struggling to assert their desires and boundaries.*

So, where did your low self-worth come from? Many factors can contribute to low self-worth, and they can vary significantly from person to person, such as rejection, bullying, abandonment, comparisons, trauma, neglect, abuse, invalidating environments, or unrealistic standards from society, parental, and authority roles. What led me to "the couch" was past experiences of rejection, abandonment from my father, and belittlement and comparison from my father's wife.

When I was young, before age 11, my father married a woman I wasn't too fond of and moved to another state. As a child, I was always okay with my mom and dad's divorce because I was too young to remember much of their marriage. Most of the things I knew were from the stories I'd heard. Before my dad married his wife, she was unkind to my sister and me. She would always say hurtful things to us when he was not around. The constant comparisons she waged between us and her youngest daughter worsened after she and my dad married and moved to another state.

According to her, her daughter was prettier than me at that age. My maternal side was so loving, validating, and affirming, so being around a woman like her was a painful adjustment. This is where my low self-esteem was formed. I would hear her say hurtful things about me to others when she thought I wasn't listening. My dad had his faults, but he always shone a light on how intelligent and pretty I was. It wasn't enough to outweigh the feelings of worthlessness and inadequacy his wife had created.

Constantly being compared to another little girl about my age made me feel as though I didn't measure up and diminished my sense of self-worth. I was too afraid to say anything to my dad because I was left alone with his wife for more time than was spent with him. Because of this, I kept quiet. He wouldn't have guessed anything was wrong because I put on the most prominent façade when he returned to his home, which I was visiting. I would be so happy for his return because, for a short time, I didn't have to endure any emotional or mental abuse. For his wife, it was almost like she would switch character when he was around. She was so sweet in his presence. I witnessed how she manipulated him. She would go from despising me and my sister to being inclusive and wanting to seem like a happy, blended family of divorcees and stepchildren.

Between my dad marrying and moving to another state without telling me, being forced to be around a woman who disliked me, my sister, and my mother, plus constantly feeling like I wasn't good enough for my dad to stay in Texas to be a father was enough to shatter the perception I had of myself. I wanted him to see that we were enough and come back to at least help raise us, but he never did. His excuse was always the cost of living. This was my first experience witnessing a man choose his life and desires over me. It was the beginning of a very desperate journey of male validation and love.

I became desperate for love. You would assume the love from my mom and my maternal side of the family would be enough to fill the voids I had, but it wasn't. The absence of a parental figure during formative years can contribute to feelings of unworthiness, insecurity, and a persistent sense of being unlovable. As children, we internalize the abandonment as a reflection of our shortcomings. This can manifest in struggles with confidence, trouble forming secure attachments, and a persistent belief we are fundamentally undeserving of love and care.

Experiencing abandonment by a parental figure causes many people to seek validation and love in their romantic relationships as a means of filling the emotional voids left by their absent parent. Because of this, their pursuit of love is usually marked by a deep-rooted fear of abandonment, leading to clingy behavior, an overwhelming need for reassurance, or a tendency to choose partners who may, more than likely, inadvertently reaffirm their feelings of unworthiness.

How Low Self-Worth Makes You Vulnerable to Manipulation

Low self-worth makes you susceptible to various forms of manipulation because it impacts your perception of yourself and your interactions with others. When you lack confidence in your own judgments, values, and abilities, you may seek validation and acceptance from external sources, making you more vulnerable to manipulation.

Your internal struggles with self-doubt and feelings of inadequacy can lead you to rely on the opinions and approval of others. As a result, you may be more inclined to comply with the desires and demands of those you perceive as having greater authority or acceptance.

The Role of the Manipulator

Manipulators are adept at identifying and exploiting other vulnerabilities for personal gain. They possess a keen ability to pinpoint and capitalize on the weaknesses of others to serve their own interests. When manipulators target people with low self-worth, they employ tactics that play on insecurities, such as offering insincere praise, creating dependency, or instilling fear of rejection. They do so knowing that these tactics may further diminish the victim's self-esteem, making them more susceptible to other manipulative tactics.

I've had to learn and teach my clients to stop letting their low self-worth dictate their pursuit of love. It's easy to fall into the trap of seeking validation from others when our self-worth is low. However, it's essential to recognize your own value and not seek validation from others. Take the time to focus on self-acceptance. We naturally attract healthier and more fulfilling relationships when we believe in ourselves and develop healthy self-esteem. This also helps us to be more aware of what love isn't. Awareness of your vulnerabilities can help you identify when someone is attempting to manipulate you. We're more capable of identifying manipulators, exploiters, and abusers.

Chapter III.
I Had Excessive Accommodation Syndrome. Just Kidding, I'm a Recovering People-Pleaser!

As expressed in Chapter I, I once had a strong compulsion to constantly seek approval and acceptance from others. What I didn't realize was that I had a fear of conflict as well. I believed that creating or entering conflict would make me susceptible to losing people I desired to have in my life. I developed this behavior as a coping mechanism in response to early experiences in my life where I felt my worth was contingent on meeting the expectations and demands of others.

As a teenager, I'd strive to excel academically to fulfill my parents' and my teachers' expectations. Whether maintaining a certain grade point average, excelling in extracurricular activities, or adhering to specific beauty standards, the need to meet these external demands often overshadowed my sense of self-worth. It felt as though my value as a person was contingent on constantly proving myself in the eyes of others. This led to a lot of anxiety, doubt, and worry.

Over time, these patterns became ingrained, leading to a chronic need to prioritize the needs of others over my own. My people-pleasing also was driven by a fear of displeasing others and fearing having to deal with the anxieties or guilt of asserting my own needs and desires. Because of this fear, I relentlessly pedestalized people who shouldn't have been on imaginary pedestals, prioritizing their comfort and happiness over my own, which took a significant toll on me mentally and emotionally.

The People-Pleasing Dilemma

The desire to please others can disrupt our personal development in our teenage years. The urge to seek approval often leads us to self-sacrifice and self-neglect. The need for acceptance and validation from our peers and authority figures becomes paramount in our adolescence, and the fear of rejection or disapproval drives us to prioritize other people's happiness over our own. This often results in us suppressing our emotions, also causing us to accept situations detrimental to our well-being.

Reflecting on my journey, I accepted several things in my people-pleasing phase. I allowed people's opinions to dictate my self-worth. I constantly molded myself to fit their expectations and lost sight of my own identity in the process.

I also had a habit of overcommitting myself to appease others. I was a "yes" girl. Me saying "yes" to every request became second nature, leaving me drained and overwhelmed. My fear of disappointing others caused me to be passive in my communication, afraid to assert my needs and advocate for myself, and struggle with setting boundaries, which led me to constantly accommodate others.

I suppressed my true feelings and emotions to keep people around and maintain harmony. My feelings found a home in a bottle I created within myself. Bottling up my feelings resulted in me being under tremendous stress and inner turmoil, which impacted my overall happiness. All of this followed me into my adult friendships and relationships. I was so easy to target. People-pleasers have certain tendencies that make it easy for manipulators to identify. Here are ways I was easy to identify as a people-pleaser:

I Over-apologized.

People pleasers often apologize excessively, even when they are not at fault. This could be for several reasons, such as trying to keep the peace, fear of rejection, loss, or abandonment, it being a chronic response from a need to seek affirmations from others, a desire to appease or pacify others, low self-esteem, a way to seek validations or reassurance from others or to avoid confrontation. I would apologize twenty times in one minute as a people-pleaser, and saying "it's okay" would not detract from my need to maintain a façade of agreeability and seek external validation. Eventually, people would make me do things to prove I was sorry; the manipulative people would. Their acceptance of my gestures made me feel "good enough" to have them in my life, which impacted my self-worth in what appeared to be a good way at that time.

I Avoided Confrontation at ALL Costs!

Looking back, I would go to great lengths to avoid confrontation, especially face-to-face disagreement. Confrontation was never my strong suit. One thing I was skilled in was strategic silence. When I sensed a potential disagreement was brewing, I would intentionally withdraw from the conversation, allowing other people to express their thoughts without interruption. It gave me time to suppress my emotions, store them in the bottle I created inside of me, and diffuse the situation.

Another method I relied heavily on as a confrontation-avoiding people-pleaser was using excuses. I became adept at creating plausible reasons to excuse myself from tense interactions. Fear caused my avoidance.

Lastly, I would cave in when a person expressed disapproval or displeasure of something I had done. I would use people-pleasing as a coping mechanism. My ongoing thoughts were, "How can I make them happy?" "How can I win their approval?" This thought process caused much emotional suffering and internal conflict.

"No" was Not a Part of my Vocabulary.

I couldn't say "no" for the life of me. If a person made a request, my answer was "yes." I struggled with setting boundaries, and part of the reason was that I felt guilty saying "no" and not being available for others because, throughout my life, I was a "yes" person and always agreed to things despite how they would affect me. And let's be honest, boundaries are usually only respected by people who don't benefit from you not having boundaries. People who have gotten away with manipulating or abusing you do not like boundaries and will push against them. That was my story. I was constantly guilt-tripped out of my boundaries. Being a person who desperately desired harmony and acceptance, setting boundaries would cause me to lose people and feel the implications of rejection, which I was not willing to experience. So, when a request was made by people, I never questioned the request or advocated for myself when it didn't align with my morals and values. Because of that, people knew I was easy to manipulate and exploit.

I Saw ME in my Client.

I sat across one of my clients I had been working with for about two months, and I couldn't help but notice familiar traits of people-pleasing that I had once struggled with myself. She was attentive to everyone's needs, always putting their desires above hers. She placed people on pedestals and abandoned herself to ensure they stayed on those imaginary pedestals. Why didn't she see her and the people she put on pedestals as equals? Was she not deserving of being on that same pedestal?

When I tried to maintain eye contact during discussions about people-pleasing, her low self-esteem and passive communication style would become easily noticeable through her inability to maintain eye contact. It was clear that her need to please others had taken a toll on her mentally and emotionally.

Drawing from my own experiences. I gently guided her to recognize the root of her people-pleasing tendencies and their impact on her life. Sometimes, your clients need to know that you understand where they're coming from. Relating to behavioral patterns that you both have experienced helps their healing process tremendously.

Together, we explored the underlying beliefs and insecurities that drove her behavior and kept her trapped in that pattern. Through a series of exercises and discussions, I helped her build a more profound sense of her self-worth and the importance of setting boundaries.

Some of the reflective questions and exercises we used can be found below. Take some time to be in solitude and honestly converse with yourself.

- **What Are My Core Beliefs?** Consider your deeply held beliefs about yourself and others. Are there beliefs that drive your desire to seek approval from others? What are the underlying assumptions or experiences that fuel your need to always say yes and avoid conflict?

- **How Do I Define Self-Worth?** Reflect on where you derive your sense of worth. Do you believe that your value comes from making others happy? How does constantly seeking approval from others impact your self-worth? What markers do you use to measure your worth, and are they based on your values or others' expectations?

- **What Are My Fear Triggers?** Identify situations or emotions that trigger your people-pleasing tendencies. Are there specific fears or anxieties that drive this behavior?

- **What Am I Afraid Of?** Explore what you fear may happen if you don't prioritize others' needs over your own. What outcomes do you worry about if you assert your own desires?

- **What Are My Relationship Patterns?** Consider your past and current relationships. Do you notice a pattern of prioritizing others' needs at your own expense?

- **What Am I Avoiding?** Evaluate whether people-pleasing serves as a way to avoid conflict, rejection, or disapproval. What discomfort are you attempting to bypass through this behavior?

- **Whose Approval Do I Seek?** Reflect on whose validation and approval hold significant influence over your actions. Are there specific individuals or groups whose acceptance feels crucial to you? How often do you prioritize other people's needs over your own?

- **What Are My Boundary-Setting Skills?** Assess your ability to set and maintain boundaries with others. Do you struggle to assert your own needs and limits? In what ways does being a people-pleaser prevent you from setting healthy boundaries? How do you feel when you think about asserting your own needs and desires in relationships and interactions?

- ❖ **What Fulfillment Do I Gain?** Examine the emotional payoff you experience from people-pleasing. What rewards do you gain from prioritizing others, such as validation or security? Are you being true to yourself in your interactions and decisions?

- ❖ **What Are My Long-Term Goals?** Consider how your people-pleasing aligns with your long-term relationships and personal growth aspirations. Are there ways this behavior hinders your progress? Can you envision a version of yourself that is liberated from the need to constantly seek approval from others? What would your life look like if you focused more on your happiness and fulfillment than pleasing others?

So, when did my people-pleasing stop? When I became exhausted. Attempting to please everyone was exhausting and unsustainable. I cared deeply for people, but realizing my naivety, empathy, and compassion were blurring my logic and being misused by people, I realized I'd lost sight of myself. I couldn't distinguish my desires from others. Only when I found myself utterly exhausted physically and emotionally did I realize something had to change. I couldn't continue to sacrifice my happiness for the sake of others. It was a hard truth to swallow, but I knew I needed to reclaim my autonomy and prioritize my needs. I deserved the prioritization and satisfaction others had experienced due to my denying and abandoning myself.

Breaking free from my people-pleasing was no easy feat. It meant setting boundaries, learning to say no, and facing the discomfort of sometimes disappointing others. But with each small step I took towards reclaiming my agency, I felt a renewed sense of empowerment and inner peace. Kindness and compassion start from within. Honoring my needs and building a more profound sense of self-respect helped me show up authentically, whether people accepted me or not. This helped me identify and weed out connections that were not good for me.

Chapter IV.
The Codependent Ties that Bind.

My codependency made me irresistible to manipulators. It seemed like no matter where I turned, I couldn't escape the cycle of falling into toxic relationships with men who thrived on controlling and exploiting my vulnerabilities. Each encounter left me feeling drained and questioning my worth, and as a result, I'd always go on a relentless pursuit of trying to prove my worth to those men. This did show up in my friendships as well.

Codependency falls on a continuum. The continuum of codependency refers to the varying degrees and manifestations of codependent behavior in relationships. People may exhibit subtle signs of emotional enmeshment and excessive caretaking at one end of the continuum. In contrast, at the other end, codependency can lead to more severe issues, such as enabling destructive behavior and a loss of one's own identity. This is the story of my early adult life.

Understanding the continuum of codependency involves recognizing the spectrum of behaviors and emotions that can characterize codependent relationships. This includes patterns of excessive reliance on validation from others, low self-worth, and a tendency to prioritize the needs of others above one's own. I recognized so much of my codependency while working with my mentor, Doc. Doc is a fantastic, retired psychologist who was still practicing when we met. I met Doc while in school. I wanted to obtain more knowledge and skills, so I sent several letters of consideration to multiple psychologists, LMFTs, counselors, etc. Many turned me down, especially within my own city. Still, Doc, who practices in a different state, called to schedule a Zoom meeting with me. To most people, Doc was intimidating, but to me, he wasn't, possibly because our personalities were similar.

I'd done extensive work on myself before training under him. Still, I displayed certain behaviors and habits from time to time under different circumstances. I'd never anticipated the revelation that was about to unfold. Being a psychologist, Doc had a keen eye for recognizing behavioral patterns, and the one day I was under a tremendous amount of stress speaking with him, he skillfully identified codependent behaviors in me. We spent over two hours reflecting on my upbringing to understand the origin of my codependency. In short, I am a child of divorced parents. I suffered from both emotional and mental abuse from the woman my father married after my mother, as well as a mother who struggled with codependency and an absent father.

Parental divorce can create many insecurities and anxieties. I witnessed my parents' relationship dismantle even after the divorce was finalized, which made me question my own stability and security. I also heard conversations I shouldn't have, which made me become an unintentional participant in my parent's emotional turmoil and conflicts. Learning the truth about why my parents divorced, knowing that my father created a lifestyle for another woman and abandoned our family, caused me to question if it was because of me and my sister and realizing he'd abandoned us. As a result, I developed a fear of abandonment, suffered from a diminished sense of self, and learned to prioritize the emotional needs of others to mitigate my fears and anxieties.

Codependency makes us more susceptible to manipulation and exploitation because it involves an excessive reliance on a relationship with another person for self-worth and identity. My codependency was characterized by people-pleasing, low self-worth, compensating with perfectionism, not advocating for myself, caretaking, enabling inexcusable harmful behaviors of others, self-sacrifice, constantly seeking validation, and needing reassurance. This is the story of many codependent people I know and clients I have helped recover from codependency.

Codependency makes us more susceptible to manipulation and exploitation because it involves an excessive reliance on a relationship with another person for self-worth and identity.

In my caretaking days, I would take on the role in an attempt to fix or rescue others. I proved my worth by always being there for people, constantly saving them from themselves or the problems they created. I felt validated by my efforts and successes in saving people. My lack of self-identity, or weak sense of self, was evident by the lengths I would go to for approval and validation from people who didn't deserve me. I enabled the destructive behaviors of people with whom I had developed fantasy bonds. I didn't know what my life was without being there for people; many needed or used me for something.

In addition to these behaviors and tendencies, I was always overinvolved in people's problems and responsibilities. Someone could vent to me about a single issue. I would put an invisible cape on my heart and take responsibility for fixing their problems. I never sat down and processed things on a less emotional level and because of that I always set myself up for failure.

I watched my mother operate in a condition to believe that her worth lied in her ability to take care of others. She would stop at nothing to be there for people. I witnessed her put herself in financial binds caring for others. I adopted this same ideology. While stemming from a genuine place of compassion, like hers, my desire to rescue and enable people caused much imbalance in my life. I failed to recognize my limitations and ultimately found myself drowning in the turmoil of other people's lives.

While working with my mentor and talking about my life's journey and processes with him, he helped me realize how my lack of boundaries and beliefs was keeping me in the same cycle of manipulative relationships. I learned my overinvolvement was not a testament to my selflessness.

Instead, it was a reflection of my own unresolved issues and insecurities. Talk about a hard pill to swallow. I was the reason I was unfulfilled. I never required anyone to fill my cup, and the false sense of security and stability I found in others was simply an illusion. I made excuses and deluded reality because of my own insecurities and fears. The realization was painful. I left that session with my mentor, feeling uneasy and sick. How did I allow myself to suffer for so long?

For me to comprehend my codependency, I had to be honest with myself and stop seeing myself as a victim. I had a skewed perception of healthy relationships. I found my worth by catering to the needs of others. I endured mistreatment from others who found their worth in using, exerting power over, and controlling me. Their sense of validation came from dominating and manipulating me to serve their own needs and desires.

In contrast, mine came from prioritizing their needs and measuring my worth based on how much I could do for them. I gave them power over my life. I validated them while invalidating myself. I offered myself as a sacrifice to the subjugation of these people. The amount of self-shame I experienced, and the guilt of failing the inner child in me was an experience I can never erase.

A New Beginning

I woke up one morning feeling strangely optimistic. It was as if a switch had been flipped in my mind, and I saw things with newfound clarity. I stood in front of the mirror and stared at myself.

It was as though I was seeing a new person right before me. I made a promise to myself that I was no longer going to be a slave to my codependent tendencies.

Just a few hours before, I received a message from my then-boyfriend: "If you are going to that doctor, you call your psychologist; you don't have to worry about me. You're probably sleeping with him, and if I find out you are, I'm going to sleep with every girl I told you not to worry about." I didn't have the energy to give to his manipulation and control. I was at peace with honoring myself. I called his phone, and before the line could connect, I was on the receiving end of being called anything vulgar he could possibly spew from his insecure mouth. After sipping my green tea and allowing him to scream for six minutes, I smiled and said, "Today is different. I wish you the best." I blocked him from my phone, social media, and emails and had my family do the same.

Understand that this took work. I had to set boundaries and maintain them. On top of that, I had to cultivate a sense of self-worth that didn't rely on other people. Breaking away from codependency was like unearthing deeply ingrained habits and thought patterns. There was an intimate relationship between my screams, tears, and pillow at night. But I was willing to put in the work. I was willing to face the discomfort and uncertainty that came with change.

Your road to breaking free from codependency may be a winding one with twists and turns you can't foresee, but taking the first step towards a life that is truly your own, a life not dictated by the needs and expectations of others, is such a liberating, fulfilling experience.

Identify the Roots of Your Codependency

Codependency can come from:

- A perfectionistic parent.
- An emotionally unstable parent.
- Inconsistent or inadequate emotional support from parents or primary caregivers.
- A parent with mental disorders, illnesses, or addictions.
- Role reversal and parentification.
- Growing up in an environment where boundaries were blurred or nonexistent.
- A codependent parent.
- An overprotective or sheltering parent.
- Child abuse, neglect, or trauma (physical, emotional, mental, verbal, or sexual)
- Parental divorce

Codependency can lead to a tendency to enable and be manipulated by others. Manipulative people exploit the vulnerabilities of people with codependent tendencies, using subtle tactics to control and influence their thoughts and actions. Understanding your codependent behaviors is paramount in identifying and thwarting manipulative behavior.

Protecting yourself starts with acknowledging and addressing your codependency and developing a healthier sense of self. Your newfound awareness will act as a defense mechanism against manipulation, exploitation, and abuse. Your discernment will disempower those who are there to use or abuse you, helping you to navigate relationships with greater clarity and autonomy. To declare yourself safe to love, you want to behave in a way that enables you to create genuine, equitable relationships. This is found in your self-worth and self-security.

Chapter V.
The Vulnerability of Empathy

Empathy and compassion are often celebrated as virtues. Still, it is crucial to acknowledge the inherent vulnerability that accompanies these traits. Empathic people genuinely desire to understand and alleviate the suffering of others. My mother and grandmother have always been the most empathic, compassionate people I've known, and unfortunately, I inherited these qualities. This is one of the ways I found myself susceptible to manipulation, exploitation, and abuse.

Empathy is your ability to experience and understand the emotions and perspectives of others. Empathic people possess a heightened sensitivity to the feelings of those around them, often placing the needs of others above their own.

Although empathy and compassion are needed to form healthy relationships and deep connections, these qualities can expose you to potential harm. If you are overly empathic and compassionate, your genuine concern for others may lead you to overlook their red flags and rationalize unacceptable behaviors. Those with malicious intent may recognize and capitalize on your empathic nature. They may use flattery, emotional manipulation, or false vulnerability to gain undue influence or control over you. You, being driven by your desire to help, may struggle to recognize when you're being exploited, placing yourself in vulnerable or potentially harmful situations.

A friend came to me some time ago about a problem. She couldn't shake the feeling of betrayal she was experiencing. This friend of mine always prided herself on her boundless empathy and compassion. Still, she realized these qualities had been used against her. The situation started innocently enough based on how she described it to me. A friend of hers came to her in a time of need. Seems as though my friend was spun a tale of woe and desperation. I'll call my friend A and her friend B for reference. My friend, A, could not ignore her friend, B's, suffering. A opened her heart and home, offering whatever support she could provide. At the time, she didn't realize that B's distress had been carefully crafted to exploit A's natural inclination to help.

As A described, the story appeared to be one I knew and lived time after time, so I was able to help her understand what was happening. As the week passed, it became clear to A that B's troubles were not as they seemed. Minor inconsistencies in the stories, subtle behavioral shifts, and a growing sense of unease all pointed to one undeniable truth: A had been manipulated.

My friend, A, always saw the best in people, but that quality had been turned against her. B took advantage of her and used A's kindness as a weapon to further her own selfish agenda. I questioned how someone could so callously exploit another person's kindness. I helped her understand that she needed to temper her empathy and compassion. These learning experiences should not harden our hearts but open our eyes. It is okay to temper your compassion with a healthy dose of skepticism; it helps protect you from calculated attempts by manipulative people.

It took A some time, but she found a new resolve once the initial shock began to wear off. We can't allow betrayal to define us. We should use our experiences of betrayal to remind us of the importance of boundaries and self-preservation.

Signs Your Empathy and Compassion May Be Being Exploited

Find yourself consistently giving support and understanding without receiving it in return or appreciating it? It may be a sign of exploitation.

You may be manipulated if a person consistently evokes guilt or pity from you to gain your assistance. Or if people exaggerate stories to elicit a desired response from you. This is a sign of emotional manipulation.

If a person consistently oversteps or disregards your boundaries, they may have ulterior motives. If you find yourself frequently uncomfortable with the requests being made of you, it could be a sign of exploitation. Exploiters typically become resistant or dismissive of the person's boundaries whom they desire to exploit or manipulate.

> *If you find yourself frequently uncomfortable with the requests being made of you, it could be a sign of exploitation.*

Suppose your empathy and compassion leave you feeling emotionally and physically depleted. In that case, it may be a sign that these qualities are being taken advantage of.

Suppose people are in constant crisis mode and continuously need support without resolution. This is a sign that you're dealing with an exploiter.

Suppose you find yourself wondering whether you are being manipulated or exploited. In that case, taking the time for introspection and evaluating your experiences is essential. Here are some of the reflective questions I use with my clients if you want to know if you're being manipulated or exploited.

1. **Do I feel pressured or coerced?** Reflect on whether you have been consistently pressured or coerced into making decisions or taking actions that don't align with your values or best interests.

2. **Are my boundaries being respected?** Consider whether your boundaries are being disregarded or if you feel uncomfortable asserting them due to fear of consequences.

3. **Am I being guilt-tripped or shamed?** Evaluate whether there is a pattern of being manipulated through guilt, shame, or emotional blackmail to control your behavior.

4. **Do I have autonomy and self-agency?** Assess whether you have the freedom to make choices independently or if your autonomy is consistently undermined.

5. **Are there imbalances of power or resources?** Examine if there are significant disparities in power dynamics or the distribution of resources within the relationship or situation.

6. **Am I being taken advantage of?** Reflect on whether your emotional, financial, or otherwise contributions are being exploited without appropriate acknowledgment or reciprocation.

7. **Is there transparency and honesty?** Consider whether there is a lack of transparency, deceit, or manipulation through misinformation or half-truths.

It can be challenging to identify when you're being manipulated. Sometimes, we subconsciously overlook manipulative behavior, especially if the manipulator is skilled at disguising their tactics. Factors such as emotional attachment, fear of confrontation, or a desire to maintain a relationship can lead us to turn a blind eye to manipulation. Additionally, you may have rationalized their behavior or attributed it to misunderstanding, choosing not to acknowledge the manipulation. Taking the time to honestly answer these questions can provide great insights into whether you are being subjected to manipulation or exploitation.

Chapter VI.
The Seeds of Doubt

As children, we are like dry sponges, ready to soak up anything the world around us has to offer. Our sense of self-worth takes shape during these formative years, influenced by the messages and experiences we receive from those closest to us.

I recall when I was about eight or nine, trying on a cute cream church dress in front of the mirror. "Y'all mama just sends y'all looking like anything," remarked my dad's wife passing by. She started praising how her youngest daughter looked, and immediately, I felt less than compared to her. I thought I looked like a princess in the dress with my hair slicked in a low ponytail, but compared to her daughter, I was nothing. I remember how those words stung, creating a ripple effect that would linger for years. The ongoing comments about my looks planted a seed of doubt in me.

I began comparing myself to every girl between the ages of eight and nineteen I would see. I became obsessed with making sure I looked like others. The need to meet societal expectations consumed me. I remember sneaking into my mother's cream foundation to make myself look prettier, like the girls in the magazines and on TV. When my mother caught me, she asked why I was playing in her makeup because my sister and I weren't allowed to do so as kids. I told her I hated myself and was ugly. The tears swelled in my mother's eyes are an image I could never forget. She sat down and had a heart-to-heart conversation with me, revealing that she suffered from low self-esteem and always tried to make sure she loved us enough to make sure we never experienced having low self-esteem. When she asked where my low self-esteem was coming from and to avoid possibly losing a connection with my dad, I didn't reveal it was his wife who made me feel that way.

My mother did everything she possibly could to reverse the doubt I had within myself, but it didn't work. I measured my worth based on how society viewed and accepted me. I needed compliments and affirmations from external sources to make me feel good about myself. Like many, my low self-worth and self-esteem came from repeated criticisms and comparisons to others. Experiences such as feelings of rejection, being bullied, unfavorable comparisons to others, perceived failure, invalidating environments, unhealthy family dynamics, lack of support, abuse, neglect, or internalization of unrealistic standards can all impact a person's self-worth, especially within the formative years.

Part of my job is to observe and identify recurring themes or patterns in my client's experiences. Over time, I have noticed a prevalent and concerning pattern of low self-worth among many individuals and couples who seek help. In our sessions,

I have witnessed how this diminished self-regard shapes their thoughts, feelings, and behaviors.

The Signs

The signs of low self-worth may not always be evident at first glance. It often manifests as a persistent sense of inadequacy, self-doubt, and a tendency to downplay or discount one's accomplishments or positive attributes. My clients who struggle with this often show perfectionistic tendencies to compensate for their feelings of inadequacy or frequently engage in constant negative self-talk, undermining their value and potential. Other signs include but are not limited to difficulty making decisions, second-guessing themselves, over-apologizing, relying on other people's approval and validation to feel worthy, being hyper-focused on their perceived flaws, going to great lengths to please others, displaying clingy or avoidant behaviors in relationships, excessively criticizing themselves when they fall short, tying their worth to the achievements, and shying away from taking risks or pursuing new opportunities.

Compensatory Actions

It's important to acknowledge that coping mechanisms for people with low self-worth vary widely and are deeply personal. Some ways that someone may attempt to compensate for negative beliefs and feelings about themselves include:

- ❖ Seeking validation and approval from others to fill the void of low self-worth could manifest as them constantly fishing for compliments and praise or making significant life decisions based on other people's opinions.

- ❖ Engaging in people-pleasing behaviors to avoid conflict and maintain a sense of acceptance.

- ❖ Placing excessive pressure on oneself to appear flawless to compensate for feelings of inadequacy. Perfectionism can manifest in various aspects of life, such as work, appearance, or relationships.

- ❖ Some people may unconsciously engage in behaviors that undermine their success and well-being. These self-sabotaging behaviors may include procrastination, avoiding opportunities to grow, or forming toxic relationships, all of which can be driven by a subconscious belief that they are undeserving of happiness or success.

- ❖ Some people may engage in escapist behaviors, seeking refuge in activities such as substance abuse, excessive gaming, or compulsive behaviors that serve as temporary distractions from negative self-perceptions.

- ❖ Over-apologizing helps them cope with a deep-seated belief that they are not worthy or deserving. This belief makes them feel responsible for any perceived wrongdoing, regardless of fault. Apologizing excessively becomes a coping mechanism to navigate their interactions, as they fear their actions may negatively impact their relationships or the acceptance they receive.

- ❖ Displaying clingy behaviors in interpersonal relationships to cope with a fear of abandonment and needing constant reassurance and validation from others. Those with low self-worth may feel unworthy of love and attention, leading them to seek continuous confirmation of their worth from their partners or friends. This clinging behavior can show up as a constant need for attention and an inability to spend time alone.

- ❖ Using avoidant behaviors to cope with negative beliefs such as disapproval from others, fear of failure, and feelings of inadequacy allows them to protect themselves from the emotional pain associated with these feelings, beliefs, and experiences. By avoiding challenges or situations that may challenge their self-image, they create a sense of safety and minimize the risk of experiencing further feelings of unworthiness. Also, avoidant behaviors help them to remain within their comfort zones, where they feel more in control and less vulnerable.

The Impact

The impact of low self-worth cannot be overstated. It permeates every aspect of your life, affecting your relationships. Low self-worth also makes you vulnerable to being targeted by people with malicious intentions. When you lack confidence in yourself and your abilities, you may be more easily swayed by the words and actions of other people. Manipulators are adept at recognizing and capitalizing on this vulnerability, using tactics that undermine your sense of self-worth and create dependency. Because of your need to be validated and accepted, you become more susceptible to flattery and manipulation. If you struggle with setting boundaries, you're more open to allowing manipulators to exploit your willingness to please and fear of rejection.

Lastly, your lack of confidence shows through your inability to trust your own judgment and make decisions. In that case, you will be more likely to overlook red flags in others. For some, low self-worth may lead to a reluctance to confront uncomfortable truths about a person or a situation. Usually, this comes from a fear of being alone or believing you do not deserve better.

It would help if you never minimized problematic behavior to maintain connections and keep people in your life. In doing so, you risk sacrificing your own well-being and self-respect. Emotional security starts within, and you must prepare to set and maintain boundaries that reflect your values. It is a courageous step to acknowledge and address problematic behaviors from manipulators and even more crucial for your growth.

Chapter VII.
No Strings Attached

A client of mine who had Dependent Personality Disorder (DPD) began to unravel the ways she had been manipulated in her toxic relationship. I gently guided her through recognizing the poisonous patterns and dynamics that governed her relationship.

My client's dependent personality disorder had made her an easy target for her boyfriend. Her constant need for reassurance and approval had created the perfect breeding ground for him, seeking to control and exploit her. She had always believed that putting others' needs above hers was a virtue, but now she saw how it had been twisted against her.

Through working with me, she had learned to identify the telltale signs of manipulation – the subtle digs disguised as jokes, the guilt trips disguised as concern, the constant demands for attention disguised as love. She had understood that true love and support didn't come with strings attached and that her worth wasn't tied to how much she could do for others.

She felt a newfound sense of clarity and empowerment as she recounted the latest manipulation incident to me. She no longer saw herself as a victim but as a survivor, reclaiming her agency and voice. With each revelation, she shed another layer of the old, submissive self and emerged more robust and resilient.

At that moment, my client realized that the path to healing wasn't easy, but it was worth it. Acknowledging the manipulation she had endured, she took the first step towards breaking free from its grip.

Dependent Personality Disorder

Dependent Personality Disorder (DPD) is characterized by an excessive need to be taken care of, leading to submissive and clinging behavior. People with this disorder often struggle to make everyday decisions without reassurance from others. They may go to great lengths to obtain support and approval. They fear being alone and feel helpless and anxious when faced with the prospect of having to be self-reliant.

People with DPD may have difficulty expressing their own opinions and needs, instead prioritizing the desires of others to avoid potential abandonment.

The Roots

The roots of DPD can be traced back to early childhood experiences, genetics, and social factors.

One significant factor is believed to be upbringing, where people with this condition may have experienced overprotective or authoritarian parenting styles hindering their ability to develop independence and self-confidence. Traumatic abandonment or withdrawn parenting can be a risk factor as well.

Genetic predisposition may also play a role if they have a family history of anxiety or personality disorders. Specific brain chemistry imbalances and neurotransmitter irregularities could contribute to the manifestation of dependent traits. Traumatic experiences during this person's formative years instill a fear of abandonment and rejection, leading to a constant need for reassurance and support from others.

The Signs

- Struggling to make everyday decisions without excessive advice or reassurance from others.

- An intense fear of being left to fend for themselves leads to clingy and submissive behavior in relationships.

- Being overly passive

- Doubting their abilities.

- Going to great lengths to avoid disagreements or conflicts to maintain the approval and support of others.

- Having a hard time functioning independently and relying on others for the most straightforward task.

- Inability to disagree with others.

- Avoiding conflict or confrontation.

- Displaying intense sadness and anxiety when experiencing a break-up, feeling abandoned, or being separated from a loved one.

- Constantly seeking relationships to avoid being alone.

- Tendency to stay in unhealthy or abusive relationships.

- Avoiding responsibilities or tasks that require independence.

- Being easily influenced or manipulated by others.

- Struggling with low self-esteem and self-worth.

- Finding it challenging to set boundaries with others.

Due to these factors, people with DPD are:

- More likely to comply with other people's wishes to avoid rejection or manipulation.

- More susceptible to being swayed by others who appear more confident or authoritative.

- ❖ Easier to exploit due to their need for approval and reassurance. Manipulators can exploit this need by providing superficial praise or support to control them.
- ❖ Taken advantage of due to their willingness to comply with people's demands.
- ❖ Self-sacrificing

Part Three
The Profile of the Manipulator

Chapter VIII.
Sharpening the Untrained Eye

Had I known what to look for to understand manipulative people's intentions and motives in the past, I could've avoided a lot of pain and emotional suffering. In our world, deception can lurk beneath the surface of seemingly innocent actions, like gifts, smiles, compliments, attention, and pursuits. Now that I have a trained eye, I can help you identify the subtle cues and hidden agendas of manipulators.

In understanding manipulators, it becomes evident that their profile is often characterized by various beliefs, experiences, influences, thought patterns, and sometimes even personality disorders. Collectively, these elements play a significant role in identifying manipulative behaviors. Understanding the profile of a manipulator can help you determine their methods and motives. This section intends to give you the knowledge needed to decipher the true intentions of those around you.

Understanding the profile of a manipulator can help you determine their methods and motives.

Understanding Manipulation

Manipulation is considered a behavior that can be pro-social (beneficial) or antisocial (harmful). Refer to the scenario examples below for reference.

Pro-Social Manipulation

Childhood: Ella, a two-year-old toddler, is playing with her best friend, Riley, in the sandbox at the park. Ella notices Riley holding a shiny toy truck she wants to play with. Instead of grabbing it forcefully, Ella comes up with a pro-social manipulation to get the toy from Riley. Ella approaches Riley with a big smile and starts complimenting him on how cool the toy truck looks and how she wishes she could play with it, too. Feeling proud of his toy, Riley offers it to Ella to play with. Ella took the opportunity and thanked Liam enthusiastically, engaging him in a cooperative play session with the toy truck. In this scenario, Ella demonstrates pro-social manipulation by using compliments and expressing her desire to play with the toy, ultimately achieving her goal of playing with it without resorting to negative behaviors like grabbing or tantrums.

Adult Relationship: Lauren noticed that her partner, Kenneth, often forgets to take breaks and relax due to work stress. Instead of nagging or telling Kenneth to take breaks, she subtly rearranged his work area by adding a comfortable chair and placing a reminder note with encouraging messages. In doing so, Lauren nudged Kenneth towards self-care without explicitly stating it.

Antisocial Manipulation

Work Relationship: Emily, a new coworker, notices that her colleague James is always eager to please and quite naive. Wanting to advance her career quickly, she exploits his trusting nature. Emily begins by praising James excessively, making him feel special and appreciated within the team. Slowly, she starts subtly undermining other colleagues in James's eyes, planting seeds of doubt about their competence and trustworthiness. As James becomes more dependent on Emily for guidance and validation, Emily starts assigning him tasks outside of his job description under the guise of mentorship. Meanwhile, she takes credit for his work and presents it as her own during team meetings.

Emily gradually isolates James from his support network by spreading rumors and manipulating situations to erode his relationships with coworkers. Ultimately, Emily secures a promotion by framing James as incompetent and unreliable to their superiors, positioning herself as the only one capable of filling his role. Unaware of the manipulation, James is left confused, alone, and unable to defend himself against the false accusations. Emily achieves her goal through calculated antisocial behavior, leaving a trail of broken trust and damaged relationships.

Dating: Ronnie and Taylor have been dating for a year. Charming and charismatic, Taylor initially swept Ronnie off her feet with lavish gifts and flattering attention. Over time, Ronnie noticed a pattern emerging - Taylor was impulsive and quick to anger when things didn't go his way, often resorting to guilt-tripping and gaslighting to maintain control. Gradually, Ronnie found herself tiptoeing around Taylor's unpredictable mood swings, feeling anxious about setting boundaries or expressing her true feelings for fear of backlash. Taylor would often play the victim, deflecting responsibility for hurtful behaviors onto Ronnie. Despite growing feelings of unease and confusion, Ronnie found it challenging to pinpoint the source of her discomfort, as Taylor could seamlessly switch between loving gestures and manipulative tactics.

As the relationship progressed, Ronnie's self-esteem diminished as she doubted her perceptions and emotions, constantly second-guessing herself. Taylor's manipulation tactics effectively isolated Ronnie from friends and family, leaving her feeling dependent and trapped in a toxic cycle of emotional distress and suffering. Despite recognizing the red flags, escaping Taylor's control seemed impossible, leaving Ronnie powerless and drained. In this scenario, you can see how seemingly charming behaviors can mask underlying toxicity and emotional abuse.

By adulthood, a person should have outgrown the manipulative tendencies from their childhood or teenage years. After a while, even if they have experienced failed relationships or trauma, they should not resort to learned behaviors of manipulation and deceit. These behaviors usually attempt to maintain the power of control within a relationship.

Chapter IX.
Cluster B "The Relationship Destroyer"

Manipulation can be a symptom of an underlying personality disorder. Certain personality disorders, such as narcissistic personality disorder, borderline personality disorder, histrionic personality disorder, or antisocial personality disorder, are commonly associated with manipulative behavior. People with these disorders may use manipulation as a means of managing their own insecurities, fears, or emotional dysregulation. Understand that people with these personality disorders don't think, reason, feel, behave, or relate to others the same as a person without these disorders.

Antisocial Personality Disorders

One of the primary characteristics of individuals with Antisocial Personality Disorder (ASPD) is a pervasive pattern of disregard for and violation of the rights of others. They may show a lack of remorse for the harm they cause others, especially after showing blatant disregard for people's boundaries. Another core feature is a pattern of deceitfulness, which can involve lying, manipulating, and conning others for personal gain. This behavior serves their self-interest, allowing them to exploit and take advantage of others without guilt or empathy. People with ASPD also tend to display impulsivity and irresponsibility, engaging in risky behaviors without considering the consequences. Lastly, people with ASPD may exhibit an inflated sense of self with a superb attitude, believing themselves to be above the rules and deserving of special treatment. This can be considered a narcissistic tendency.

People with Antisocial Personality Disorder (ASPD) have a distinct emotional pattern that presents difficulties in forming genuine connections with others and understanding social cues related to emotions. They may lack empathy and express shallow emotions as they struggle to understand or relate to the feelings of others. They also may struggle to experience deep emotional responses and outwardly display emotional detachment. You might notice that they're also impulsive and act on impulse or engage in risky behaviors without considering the consequences of their actions. Due to their impulsive and irresponsible nature, they may also struggle with fulfilling responsibilities or obligations. They may display a pattern of aggression, hostility, and irritability, manifesting in verbal and physical altercations. Due to their manipulative and abusive nature, they typically destroy relationships and the people they make fictitious connections with.

Borderline Personality Disorder

Borderline Personality Disorder (BPD) is characterized by a pattern of instability in interpersonal relationships, self-image, and emotions. One core personality feature is people with BPD often have an overwhelming fear of being abandoned or rejected by others. Because of this, they may engage in frantic, manipulative efforts to avoid real or imagined abandonment. Another feature is they may frequently engage in impulsive behaviors to cope with intense emotions or to alleviate feelings of emptiness. They experience intense and rapidly shifting emotions such as extreme sadness, anger, or anxiety that can escalate quickly and be challenging to regulate.

Because of their unstable self-image, they typically struggle with a distorted sense of self that leads to feelings of emptiness and identity confusion, making it difficult to understand their own values, goals, and preferences. People with BPD often have tumultuous and unstable relationships characterized by idealization and devaluation; because of this, they may alternate between intense adoration and disdain for others, leading to frequent conflicts and difficulties maintaining long-term connections.

Also, people with BPD may struggle with distinguishing between reality and fantasy, causing them to experience brief episodes of dissociation of paranoia, impacting their perception of the world around them. Lastly, they may struggle to manage feelings of anger, leading to frequent outbursts or episodes of rage. This pattern of dysregulation and outward expressions strain relationships.

Narcissistic Personality Disorder

Narcissistic Personality Disorder (NPD) is characterized by a pattern of grandiosity, a need for admiration, and a lack of empathy. People with NPD typically have an exaggerated sense of self-importance, leading them to constantly seek admiration and believe they're superior to others. Hence, the reason they usually target people who struggle with self-worth, have codependent tendencies or are people-pleasers. A person with this disorder has a strong need for validation from others as well. Praise and approval help to boost their self-esteem. Codependents or people-pleasers often change the dynamic of their relationship by placing another person on an imaginary pedestal; narcissistic personality disorders take advantage of them.

One of the critical traits of NPD is their struggle to recognize or understand other people's emotions or perspectives. They believe they are entitled to special privileges and may expect others to cater to their needs and desires. Their exploitative behaviors lead them to exploit others to achieve their goals. They may manipulate or exploit others without guilt or remorse.

Histrionic Personality Disorder

Like the other Cluster B disorders, people with Histrionic Personality Disorder (HPD) exhibit a range of distinct characteristics that shape their personality and interactions with others. They display attention-seeking behavior and may go to great lengths to be noticed. When not the center of attention, they may feel uncomfortable. They may display exaggerated or dramatic emotions, which can fluctuate rapidly. Their feelings may seem shallow or lack depth, leading to a tendency to overreact to situations.

Also, people with HPD might engage in flirtatious or seductive behavior to maintain the interest of others. They'll use their physical appearance and charm to captivate and manipulate others. They need approval and usually struggle with rejection. Like Antisocial Personality Disorder, they may act impulsively, engage in reckless behaviors, struggle to respect their own and other people's personal boundaries and have a blurred sense of what is socially appropriate.

What you should have identified by now is there is a pattern amongst all Cluster B personality disorders. One specific pattern is them displaying manipulative behaviors to achieve their desired outcomes or to cope with their emotions. In relationships with someone exhibiting traits of a Cluster B disorder, manipulation can be subtle and insidious, making it challenging for the victim to recognize and address.

The Social Chameleon

Bearing traits reminiscent of narcissistic, antisocial, borderline, and histrionic personality disorder, the social chameleon uses manipulative tactics such as guilt-tripping, gaslighting, control, and coercion. They evaluate their potential victim's/partner's gullibility and naivety, altering their presentation afterward to what is deemed to be the most effective. They will study their victims to see how they should temper their personalities in a way where they'll quickly be accepted by their victims and gain the access they desire. They'll threaten to harm themselves or may actually hurt themselves to retain their partner using guilt and obligation.

The Loser

The Loser is a player skilled in manipulation. They usually have two lives, one that is their real life and the other that is fantastic. Their imaginary life is typically full of excuses, deception, lies, half-truths, and extreme stories. They usually have conspiracy theories about their lives, blaming others for their circumstances to absolve themselves of personal responsibility. You may witness them verbally expressing the great talents and potential they possess. Still, you may also notice they have little to no social or occupational success.

Also, they'll make promises that never take place. The most significant indicator you're dealing with a loser is them needing you to do things for them, such as getting cars, homes, apartments, accounts, or businesses in your name. Their lives are usually accompanied by financial irresponsibility, constant job loss, legal struggles, or frequent living from house to house or with others. Their stories are so convincing that even the most discerning mind can become trapped in their façade. Their victim mentality, evident by their need for sympathy and pity from others, is commonly used to manipulate others into enabling them.

The Situationally Moral Manipulator

The situationally moral manipulator lives by two mottos: "Do what I have to do" and "The end justifies the means." They suffer from situational moralism marked by their attitude of meeting their needs at the expense of other people's sanity. They don't feel bound by societal rules or morals.

Also, their ideology that the end justifies the means requires morally questionable tactics. This mindset can be dangerous and unethical as they rationalize increasingly unethical behaviors in pursuit of their desired outcome. They don't hesitate to harm themselves or tarnish their reputation or the reputations of others to get their needs met. Manipulative tools are often tools of the trade, such as conning, lying, intimidation, coercion, scheming, and pretentious behavior.

The Shallow Player

The shallow players, marked by shallow emotions, lack of remorse, and emotional detachment, often have limited investment in their victims and partners, as their actions are driven by self-interest rather than genuine care or concern for others. They demonstrate minimal investment in their partners or victims, only exerting effort when their victim's demands are minimal. Their involvement is superficial, showing disinterest in exceeding the basic requirements. When the demands become too high, it's easier for them to dispose of someone and move on to another. They'll do the same to the new victim unless that person's demands remain low, which usually calls for that person to abandon themselves. If their behaviors are criticized, they'll move on. They'll move on if you're too needy or troublesome to them. You're only valuable when they need you, not when you need them. Suppose you've experienced this type of manipulator. You may have noticed they move on quickly and usually can find another partner following a breakup, sometimes within days.

The Talk a Good Game Manipulator

Their words are marked by empty promises, and their actions are illusions. The manipulator who talks a good game usually has a gap between their words and actions. Honest people have conversations or make promises that match their behaviors almost always. On the other end, there are dishonest people who frequently and consistently drop the ball, making it harder to trust them. Their words speak louder than their actions, showing how unfair and unreliable they are. For example, a person telling you they love you and will never hurt you but continues to gossip about you or spread lies about you, in fact, shows the gap between their words and actions. Another example is a partner who has previously been caught cheating and assures you they will no longer cheat but continues to cheat and tries to justify their behavior, showing there was no intention to fulfill that promise. For this reason, judging people by their behavior and actions is more important than their talk.

Their words are marked by empty promises, and their actions are illusions. The manipulator who talks a good game usually has a gap between their words and actions.

Unconscious Behavior or Calculated Behavior?

Manipulators, exploiters, abusers, or Cluster B personalities are all often associated with manipulative behaviors. Whether these behaviors are unconscious or calculated can vary depending on the person and the specific circumstances.

Some behavior may be unconscious. For example, a person with narcissistic personality disorder may manipulate others as a way to fulfill their own needs for validation and admiration without fully realizing the impact of their actions on others. Similarly, people with borderline personality disorder may engage in manipulative behaviors as a means of regulating their intense emotions or fears of abandonment.

On the other hand, some manipulation can be calculated. For instance, those with antisocial personality disorder may deliberately manipulate others for personal gain or to exploit their trust. They may use charm and deceit to manipulate situations to their advantage, demonstrating a level of planning and awareness of the consequences of their actions.

Manipulators may employ tactics such as gaslighting and distorting reality to sow seeds of doubt in their target's mind. Through carefully calculated words and actions, they'll twist the truth, undermining their target's confidence and making them more susceptible to manipulation. Charm and flattery from these manipulators are used to disarm their victims, drawing them in before asserting control. Manipulators may also use selective information sharing, revealing only bits and pieces of the truth to control how others perceive a situation.

> *Manipulators may also use selective information sharing, revealing only bits and pieces of the truth to control how others perceive a situation.*

Furthermore, exploiters are skilled at exploiting their victim's emotional vulnerabilities, using guilt, fear, or empathy to sway opinions. They observe and analyze their target's behaviors and emotions to tailor their approach to eliciting their desired response.

Manipulative people use calculated behaviors characterized by strategic planning, emotional manipulations, and insidious tactics to secure their objectives.

How is a Manipulator's Attitude Formed?

A manipulator's attitude is often shaped by internal and external factors. Internally, manipulators may have deep-seated insecurities, driving them to exploit others for personal gain. They may have experienced past traumas or setbacks that have influenced their view of others and the world around them. This affects how they relate to others, as they may use manipulative behaviors as a coping mechanism.

Externally, their upbringing, social influences, and past experiences can significantly shape their attitude. Growing up in an environment where manipulation is normalized or rewarded can teach them that deceit and exploitation are acceptable means to achieve their goals or have their desires met. They have an impaired way of relating to other people. It doesn't matter how socially skilled, loving, warm, caring, empathetic, or accepting you are with them; their defective social style will continue.

Listening to people's stories about their past relationships, family, upbringing, and circumstances, as well as paying attention to who they associate themselves with and how they respond in social situations or under social pressures, can help you identify any signs of manipulation or exploitation that can caution how you proceed with them.

Their decision-making, coping mechanisms, and manipulative behaviors are often planned to meet their agenda. Their long-standing behavioral patterns, plus their calculated behaviors, make them dangerous and leave a trail of suffering, insecurities, and trauma within their victims.

Part Four
The Manipulator's Playbook

Chapter X.
Tactics & Strategies

It would be best to familiarize yourself with manipulation tactics to protect yourself from falling victim to them. By being aware, you can recognize when someone is attempting to manipulate you and take necessary steps to safeguard your emotions and well-being.

Understanding these tactics can help you create and maintain healthier relationships. If you can identify signs of manipulation early on, you can address any issues directly and establish healthy boundaries. Knowing these tactics also enhances your decision-making skills as you can approach situations with a more critical eye, analyzing information objectively and also helping you evaluate potential hidden agendas. This heightened awareness empowers you to make informed choices that align with your values and goals, free from external influence.

Manipulators operate in the shadows and prefer to operate under the radar, avoiding detection of their tactics and behaviors. Revealing their manipulative tactics would undermine their power and influence on their victims, making it harder for them to manipulate others in the future.

If people become educated about manipulative behaviors, they are more likely to recognize and resist these tactics, threatening the manipulator's agenda. Manipulators rely on secrecy and deception to maintain their advantage, making it crucial for them to prevent others from learning about their harmful strategies.

In this section of the book, my aim is to equip you with the tools necessary to identify the strategies employed by manipulative, exploitative, or abusive people. From gaslighting and guilt-tripping to flattery and playing the victim, we will shine a light on the subtle, yet harmful ways manipulators operate.

My hope is that by the end of the section, you will have developed a keen sense of awareness when it comes to spotting manipulation in all forms.

Gaslighting

This tactic involves the manipulator denying or altering the target's perception of reality, making the victim question their sanity or memory.

Example: A wife repeatedly denies things she previously said or did, causing her husband to doubt his memory or perception of events.

Example: A friend promises to attend an event but later claims they never agreed to, making the other friend question their recollection of the conversation.

Guilt-Tripping

Manipulators use guilt to make their target feel responsible for their unhappiness, problems, or circumstances, thereby pressuring the target into compliance.

> *Manipulators use guilt to make their target feel responsible for their unhappiness, problems, or circumstances, thereby pressuring the target into compliance.*

Example: A dating prospect reaching out to a person of interest who is out of town with friends sending a text that says:

Hey! I know you're out of town, but I hoped we'd catch up this weekend. You must be too busy with your friends. It's OK, I understand. I just thought it would be nice to spend time together since we haven't seen each other in a while. But hey, I'm used to being the one who always has to reach out. It's OK, really. I'll just be here, waiting for you to make time for me like I always do for you. Just remember that I'm always here for you, even if you're too busy for me. No pressure though!

Love-bombing

This strategy involves the manipulator overwhelming the target with attention, affection, nice gestures, and praise to create a dynamic of dependency and control on the target.

Example: Tori meets Kevin at a networking event. Kevin showers Tori with constant attention, gifts, and affection from the very beginning. He floods her with messages professing his love and admiration, making grand romantic gestures, and planning extravagant dates. At first, Tori is swept off her feet by Kevin's overwhelming displays of affection and flattery. However, as time goes on, she starts to feel suffocated. She realizes that Kevin's love-bombing is not sincere but a tactic to gain her trust and manipulate her emotions. He attempted to move the relationship unusually fast, talking about their future together within two months. He'd also try to guilt-trip her into reciprocating his feelings, making her feel obligated to respond to his advances the way he desired.

Isolation

Manipulators may isolate their target from their social circle of family, friends, or support networks, making the target easier to control and influence.

Example: A boyfriend convinces his girlfriend that her friends and family are untrustworthy and tries to sabotage their relationship when they're trying to help make the girlfriend aware of his unfaithful behavior.

Example: A wife monitors and controls her husband's communication, constantly scrutinizing his interactions with others. She might withhold affection or give the silent treatment until he complies and limits his access to his friends.

Negging

This manipulative tactic involves the manipulator giving backhanded compliments or subtle insults to undermine their target's self-esteem and increase their reliance on the manipulator for validation.

Example: Imagine your crush, who knows you are interested in them, approaches you and says, "You seem pretty cool for someone who doesn't really dress up." This seemingly backhanded compliment is intended to make you feel self-conscious about your appearance while appearing superior. It can be disguised as playful teasing but aims to make you seek validation from them. You may dress up more or conform to what you believe would be approved by them.

Pulling the Victim Card or Playing Victim

Manipulators may portray themselves as victims or garner sympathy, pity, or recognition from their target, usually deflecting accountability or justifying their behaviors.

Example: Every disagreement between Yolanda and Paul turned into a tale of how Yolanda mistreated Paul. During their latest argument about household chores, Paul once again twisted the conversation to make Yolanda the villain. When Yolanda would try to explain her perspective, Paul would make attempts to cry, conveying a sense of hurt. This would cause Yolanda to be overcome by guilt and doubt her frustrations. She'd ask herself if she was being too harsh or expecting too much of Paul, knowing deep down about Paul's habit of playing the victim. His resorting to pulling the victim's card had clouded her judgment, using it to deflect accountability and to avoid addressing his shortcomings in their relationship.

Silent Treatment

Manipulators or abusers might intentionally ignore or withhold communication to exert control and instill anxiety in their target.

Example: Imagine a couple going from laughing daily to barely speaking to one another, passing each other without saying a word. There's still unresolved tension from the last conflict, and the weight of their words is still hanging in the air. The boyfriend's attempt to connect proves themselves to be unsuccessful. He lies awake in his bed beside her, replaying the last argument, searching for clues to figure out where it went wrong. His girlfriend's silence spoke volumes where words failed, pushing them further apart.

Triangulation

Manipulators will bring a third party into their dynamic to create jealousy, insecurity, comparison, or competition, consolidating their position of power.

Example: Cayden's narcissistic mom, Rebecca, constantly undermines his fiancé's confidence and belittles her accomplishments in front of Cayden. She makes subtle comments that Nya,

Cayden's fiancé, isn't good enough for him, leading Nya to feel insecure and doubtful of her place in the engagement. Cayden goes along with his mother's manipulative behavior by not defending Nya or setting boundaries with his mom. Instead, he oscillates between showing affection to Nya and siding with his mother, creating confusion and turmoil for Nya.

As a result, Nya feels isolated, anxious, and unsure of who to trust, leaving her vulnerable to further manipulation.

Selective Truth-telling

Manipulators may selectively reveal or withhold information to control the narrative and shape their target's perceptions.

Example: Consider this scenario, in a negotiation meeting, a teammate highlights the positive aspects of a deal while conveniently leaving out any drawbacks or risks involved. They can influence the other teammate's decisions by strategically shaping the narrative with partial truths without outright lying.

Threats and Intimidation

Manipulators may use fear and coercion to compel compliance or silent dissent from their target.

Fear-mongering: Manipulators may utilize threats, exaggerations, or a sense of impending danger to instill fear and compliance in their target.

Example: An abuser threatens physical harm and makes intimidating gestures to keep their victim compliant and afraid to speak out. They also employ gaslighting techniques to distort reality and make their victim doubt their own perceptions, exacerbating feelings of fear and confusion. They isolate their victim from friends and family, creating a sense of dependency and fear of being abandoned. These fear-driven behaviors are designed to maintain control and dominance over their victim.

Bullying: Manipulators use bullying to undermine their target's self-esteem and autonomy. They may criticize and use belittling remarks to break their target's confidence.

Projection

Accusing the target of behaviors or motives that the manipulator possesses deflects the attention away from the manipulator's actions, creating confusion in the target.

Example: Liam has been unfaithful to Taylor multiple times, but instead of acknowledging his actions, he starts projecting his guilt onto Taylor. One evening, Taylor innocently asks Liam about his day, unaware of the affair that took place earlier. Feeling guilty and defensive, Liam immediately accuses Taylor of being distant and secretive. He starts gaslighting Taylor, claiming that she must be cheating because she has been working late and spending time with friends.

Subtle Power Plays

Manipulators may create subtle hierarchies to control the target, such as managing resources or withholding information.

Example: Chrissy is the primary breadwinner and controls the household finances. Don, who relies on Chrissy for financial support, gradually finds himself in a vulnerable position where his choices and autonomy are limited.

Chrissy's control of finances dictates how money is spent within their relationships, creating a sense of obligation and indebtedness in Don. Because of this power dynamic, Chrissy influences decisions on where they live, what they buy, and how their time is spent.

Control

Manipulators may use control as a coping mechanism when they feel insecure or overwhelmed. By manipulating their target, they create a sense of stability and predictability in their lives, thus alleviating their anxiety.

Example: Abby befriended Tamara, a well-known and charismatic girl in their town. Over time, Abby noticed subtle shifts in their interactions as Tamara became controlling in their friendship. Tamara would often criticize Abby's choices. Behind closed doors, Tamara would confide in Abby about her own insecurities, manipulating Abby into providing constant reassurance and validation.

As Tamara's insecurities grew, so did her need to control Abby. She would guilt-trip Abby into spending more time with her and sharing personal information. Slowly, Abby distanced herself from other friends and family at Tamara's insistence. Tamara's manipulation had turned Abby into a constant source of support, feeding Tamara's fragile ego and insecurities.

Unbeknownst to Abby, Tamara's need for control stemmed from her deep-seated fear of being abandoned and unloved. By exerting dominance over Abby, Tamara found a temporary escape from her insecurities, clinging to the power she held in their lopsided relationship.

Minimizing

This tactic is used by manipulators to downplay or trivialize their target's feelings or experiences. It causes the target to question their own emotions and reality.

Example: When Zayne receives a job promotion, her boyfriend, Alan, initially reacts less enthusiastically than she hoped for. He commented that the promotion might mean more extended hours and more stress, downplaying the significance of her achievement; as Zayne spoke more about her promotion, Alan shifted the conversation towards his own work challenges, implying that his job was more demanding and stressful than hers.

Over time, Zayne noticed a pattern where Alan consistently downplayed her achievements, leading her to doubt herself and feel unsupported.

Blaming or Blame-shifting

Manipulators often shift blame to deflect responsibility from themselves onto their target. It helps them to preserve their self-image, avoid consequences, garner sympathy from those around them, and maintain control.

Example: One partner forgets about a significant event; they shift the blame by saying the other partner didn't remind them enough.

Changing Criteria

A manipulator can control the outcome to suit their agenda by constantly shifting the standards or requirements. This leads the target to doubt their judgment or feel inadequate when they can't meet the manipulator's ever-changing expectations or keep up.

Example: Jason and Sam have been in a relationship for over a year now. At the beginning of their relationship, Sam clarified that honesty was the most important value for her as a partner. Jason, wanting to impress Sam, showed her that he was honest in their relationship.

Sam began to change her criteria for what mattered most to her as time passed. Suddenly, it wasn't just about honesty anymore but also about

Jason's time with her. She started commenting about feeling neglected and unloved whenever Jason wanted to spend time with his friends or focus on his work. Slowly, Jason noticed that Sam's approval and affection were directly tied to how much time he dedicated to her. Feeling trapped and manipulated, he sacrificed his personal time and interests to keep Sam happy. By shifting the goalposts of what is deemed necessary, Sam exerts control over Jack and uses his desire to please her as a tool for manipulation.

Generalizations

Manipulators use this tactic to oversimplify issues or people. By making broad, sweeping statements, manipulators can steer conversations in their favor. They may use tactics to stereotype or pigeonhole their target, making it easier to control influence perceptions.

Example: Kayla consistently accuses Joseph of "always prioritizing work over our relationship." This generalization ignores the times when Joseph tried to balance work and their relationship.

Name-calling

Used to degrade or belittle their target, manipulators use name-calling to assert power and control over them. This tactic diminishes their target's self-worth and esteem, weakening the target's position in the conflict or argument.

Example: During a heated argument, one partner raises their voice and starts calling the other partner hurtful names like "stupid" or "worthless." This type of behavior can cause deep emotional pain in the person on the receiving end of the name-calling.

Changing the Subject

Manipulators change the subject to deflect away from a topic or issue the target wants to address directly. They can maintain control and avoid confrontation or accountability by sidestepping the current subject and redirecting the conversation elsewhere.

Example: Imagine a scenario where Dayna is being confronted about a problematic behavior she exhibited. Instead of acknowledging her actions and taking responsibility, she might swiftly transition the discussion to an unrelated topic to deflect attention from her behavior. This tactic derails the original conversation and sidesteps any potential repercussions or accountability the individual should face.

Passive-Aggressiveness

Passive aggressiveness is a form of manipulative behavior where a person may express their negative feelings subtly or indirectly. Instead of openly addressing conflicts or issues, they employ tactics such as sarcasm, silent treatment, or subtle sabotage to convey their unhappiness. When a manipulative person says something indirectly or without outright saying what they mean, it keeps the victim in a constant pattern of guessing, monitoring, hypervigilance, or trying to anticipate or adjust to the manipulator's moods and responses.

When a manipulative person says something indirectly or without outright saying what they mean, it keeps the victim in a constant pattern of guessing, monitoring, hypervigilance, or trying to anticipate or adjust to the manipulator's moods and responses.

Example: Imagine a scenario where one partner consistently agrees to do tasks or favors for the other but carries them out inefficiently or with intentional mistakes. This behavior can express underlying resentment or assert control covertly without overtly addressing the issue.

Dismissiveness

Displayed as an attitude of superiority or indifference, manipulators attempt to diminish the validity of their target's perspective, leading the target to question their own worth and beliefs.

Example: Imagine a scenario where one partner constantly dismisses the other's concerns or emotions as unimportant or irrational.

The dismissive partner might use phrases like "You're overreacting" or "You're being too sensitive" to belittle the other person's feelings. By invalidating their emotions, the manipulative partner can gain control over the relationship dynamics and avoid addressing any issues that make them uncomfortable.

Over time, the person receiving this dismissive behavior may start doubting themselves and their perceptions. They might begin second-guessing their emotions and hesitating to express their true thoughts, ultimately giving the manipulative partner more power and influence.

Infantilizing their Target

Manipulators use this tactic to control their target, treating them as if they are much younger or less capable than they actually are. This can appear as the manipulator speaking to their target condescendingly, making decisions on their behalf without consulting or belittling their abilities.

Example: Jonathan frequently treats Bria like a child, making decisions on her behalf without consulting her opinion. He dismisses her thoughts and feelings, often speaking over her in conversations and disregarding her input. Bria's attempts to assert herself are met with condescending remarks and gestures, leaving her feeling powerless and insignificant in the relationship.

Through subtle manipulations and controlling behaviors, Johnathan reinforces a dynamic where Bria is made to feel incompetent and reliant on him for validation and guidance.

DARVO Strategy

The **DARVO** strategy is to **Deny, Attack, and Reverse the Victim and Offender**. It is often used by those confronted with an accusation to flip the narrative in their favor.

Deny: The first step involves denying the allegation outright. Refuting the claim, the person attempts to create doubt and sow confusion.

Attack: Next, the accused person may launch a counterattack against the accuser. This could involve discrediting the person making the accusation or shifting the focus onto their motives or actions instead.

Reverse Victim and Offender: In this final stage, the person reverses the roles of victim and offender. By portraying themselves as the actual victim, they seek to garner sympathy and deflect attention away from the original issue.

Other behaviors include humiliation, accusations, and pretending not to understand what you're saying. Understanding a manipulator's tactics can help protect yourself against potential harm and deception. Manipulators often prey on people who are unaware of their strategies. They also frequently blur boundaries and disregard personal limits to serve their agenda. By being attuned to red flags and manipulative behaviors, you can make informed choices and avoid deception-influenced decisions. Equipping yourself with the knowledge of a manipulator's tactics is not about breeding mistrust or paranoia but empowering yourself to navigate interpersonal interactions with discernment and resilience.

Part Five
To Overcome and Empower

Chapter XI
Consequences of Being Manipulated or Psychologically Abused

Manipulation can significantly impact the brain, leading to psychological consequences. Repeated manipulation can cause changes in brain function. If you've been a victim of manipulation in the past, you may have experienced heightened levels of stress, leading to an increase in cortisol, the stress hormone. We, as humans, are not supposed to be under significant stress for long periods of time. This disrupts the functioning of the brain region responsible for processing emotions and the area responsible for decision-making and judgment.

Constant manipulation causes you to question your perceptions and judgment, eventually diminishing your self-confidence. You become more dependent on external validation and less trusting of your instincts. Also, prolonged stress from constant manipulation can contribute to many health issues, including cardiovascular problems, insomnia, headaches, stomach issues, and a weakened immune system.

Constant manipulation causes you to question your perceptions and judgment, eventually diminishing your self-confidence.

You may become more isolated with a dysfunctional view of the world. You may feel like you're always walking on eggshells from constantly being in a state of hypervigilance and monitoring, never knowing what may trigger a negative response in the manipulative or abusive person. A constant state of hypervigilance can disrupt your ability to regulate your emotions. Due to the amygdala, the region of the brain responsible for processing emotions being impacted, you may have intense feelings of fear, anxiety, and a distorted sense of reality.

Over time, you can develop symptoms of trauma, such as hypervigilance, flashbacks, nightmares, and difficulty trusting others. Being manipulated also can put you in a vicious cycle of negative thought patterns and behavioral responses. You may experience intense feelings of guilt and shame, even though you are not at fault for the psychological abuse you have endured. Your thoughts may race as you try to understand what has happened and what you have suffered; this is a typical response.

Learning what makes you vulnerable to manipulation does not mean that it is your fault. Again, being manipulated is not your fault. It's natural to want to trust others and believe in the good intentions of those around you. However, regardless of intelligence or strength, manipulation can happen to anyone. It's important to remember that the manipulator is the one in the wrong, not you. You are not to blame for someone else's deceptive behavior.

Chapter XII
Outsmarting the Manipulator

So far, you've learned what makes you vulnerable and susceptible to manipulation; you have also gained knowledge of a manipulator's profile and tactics playbook. This should help you feel more confident in outsmarting a manipulator. We can take a few more steps to help you move forward.

Recognize the Signs

Pay attention to subtle cues such as guilt-tripping, gaslighting, inconsistencies between words and actions, or constant lying to identify manipulative behavior.

Stay Calm and Rational

Manipulators thrive on evoking emotional responses. Stay composed and think logically to avoid falling into their traps. The best way to respond to a manipulator is to not react as they want you to. Eventually, you'll become a boring subject to them and useless, which is good for you.

Know Your Values and Set Boundaries

Knowing your values is essential when setting boundaries with a manipulator. When you are clear on what you stand for and believe in, you have a solid foundation to draw from when faced with manipulative tactics. You can recognize when a manipulator tries manipulating you into crossing a line and respond accordingly. Clearly communicate your boundaries and stick to them. Manipulators often test limits to see how much they can control a situation.

Trust Your Instincts

If something feels off or too good to be true, take a step back and reassess the situation. You've learned manipulators often use charm and charisma to deceive others, appearing friendly and approachable on the surface, with a hidden agenda underneath.

Document Interactions

Keep a record of conversations or agreements to prevent manipulation tactics like twisting words or denying promises. This proactive approach serves as a reliable reference point to address any discrepancies or attempts made by a manipulator to distort the truth.

Talk to Someone You Can Trust

Talking to a trusted friend, family member, or therapist about your concerns can be beneficial. They can offer an outside perspective to validate your feelings and guide you. Be open, transparent, and honest, as they can provide support and insight you may not have considered. Consider reaching out to someone who can offer a listening ear and a different point of view to help you navigate your concerns.

Be Assertive

Stand firm in your beliefs and decisions. Practice saying no and asserting your needs to build resilience against manipulation. It is okay to prioritize your own needs and values, even if it means going against the expectations of others.

Limit Contact

Reduce interactions with the manipulator to minimize their influence over you. By reducing engagement with manipulative people, you can safeguard yourself and prevent their tactics from affecting you as strongly.

Focus On Yourself

Manipulators may target your vulnerabilities, preying on your insecurities. Make it a priority to participate in activities that nourish your soul and bring you peace. Taking care of yourself is essential in outsmarting them.

> **Stay mindful, stay grounded,
> and stay true to yourself.**

Letter from Kittie

You're not responsible or to blame for their lies, deceptions, or behavior. It doesn't matter if you were present; they would still exhibit manipulative tendencies. Manipulation, exploitation, and abuse are inherent to them. It would not alter their behavior even if you were to change everything about yourself. Your alterations would merely cater to their demands and inadvertently validate their actions. Love alone cannot transform them. Chances are you're not the first person who believed that loving them could induce a change in them. You could love a shark, but it would not change its innate instinct to attack when it detects blood. If you are waiting for a transformation, stop. Time will not reform them. Do not justify their inexcusable behaviors. Having a baby, moving in together, or getting married won't resolve anything either. Instead, these stressors will likely exacerbate their dysfunctional behaviors and amplify their traits. Tonight, strive to love yourself a little more. You should take pride in where you are. The fact that you have nurtured a desire to alter your circumstances is commendable, and I celebrate this for you.

I wish you the best. Happy healing and happy, healthy relationships.

Sincerely,

Kittie J. Rose

Printed in Great Britain
by Amazon